Dear Parent:
Your child's love of reading starts here!

Every child learns to read in a different way and at his or her own speed. Some go back and forth between reading levels and read favorite books again and again. Others read through each level in order. You can help your young reader improve and become more confident by encouraging his or her own interests and abilities. From books your child reads with you to the first books he or she reads alone, there are I Can Read Books for every stage of reading:

SHARED READING
Basic language, word repetition, and whimsical illustrations, ideal for sharing with your emergent reader

BEGINNING READING
Short sentences, familiar words, and simple concepts for children eager to read on their own

READING WITH HELP
Engaging stories, longer sentences, and language play for developing readers

READING ALONE
Complex plots, challenging vocabulary, and high-interest topics for the independent reader

ADVANCED READING
Short paragraphs, chapters, and exciting themes for the perfect bridge to chapter books

I Can Read Books have introduced children to the joy of reading since 1957. Featuring award-winning authors and illustrators and a fabulous cast of beloved characters, I Can Read Books set the standard for beginning readers.

A lifetime of discovery begins with the magical words "I Can Read!"

Visit www.icanread.com for information
on enriching your child's reading experience.

To Wes and Anne, with love
—B.H.

For Mattie
—G.F.

I Can Read Book® is a trademark of HarperCollins Publishers.

Library of Congress Control Number: 2018942095
ISBN 978-0-06-227917-0 (trade bdg.) — ISBN 978-0-06-227916-3 (pbk.)

Typography by Erica De Chavez
18 19 20 21 22 SCP 10 9 8 7 6 5 4 3 2 1 ❖   First Edition

I Can Read!

BEGINNING 1 READING

CLARK THE SHARK
TOO MANY TREATS

WRITTEN BY BRUCE HALE   ILLUSTRATED BY GUY FRANCIS

HARPER

An Imprint of HarperCollinsPublishers

"I can't wait for tomorrow!"
said Clark the Shark.
"What's tomorrow?"
asked Benny Blowfish.

"It's Treats Tuesday," said Clark.

"And my mom's baking brownies!"

"My mom's brownies are so yummy,
they thrill my tummy!"
Clark told Amanda Eelwiggle.

"Sounds great," said Amanda.

"Mom's brownies are so sweet,
they can't be beat!"
Clark told Joey Mackerel.
"Have I said how much I love them?"

"Oh, once or twice," said Joey.

Clark told everyone in class
about his mom's brownies.
Soon all Clark's friends were
hungry for them. . . .

Even Clark's teacher, Mrs. Inkydink, couldn't wait.

After school, Clark hurried home.

And what did he see on the counter?

Fresh-baked brownies!

Yum-yum-YUM!

"Mom, can I try one?" he called.

But Clark's mom had gone shopping.

He stared at the brownies.

"Someone should test them," he said,

"to make sure they're okay."

Clark ate one brownie.

"WOW!" said Clark. "That's tasty!"

He eyed the dish.

Sure, ONE brownie was good.

But how could he know

if the others were, too?

16

"Maybe just one more," said Clark.

So Clark ate another brownie.

"That's yummy, too!" he said.

He eyed the dish again.

Sure, those two brownies were good.

But what about the rest?

"I can't let my classmates down!"

So Clark ate another brownie.

And another . . .

and another.

Pretty soon, they were all gone.

Then Clark's mother came home.

"You're in trouble now!"

said Clark's brother, Mark.

Clark's mom was upset.

"How could you?!" she asked.

"After all my hard work?"

"I'm so sorry," said Clark.

"I couldn't stop eating."

"One brownie is fine," she said.

"But when you've had your snack,
just hold back."

"I'll remember that," said Clark.

Clark baked a new batch of brownies
(with a little help from Mom).
And when they cooled off,
he added some fancy decorations.

At school the next day,

everyone loved the brownies.

"Yum-yum-yum!" said Billy-Ray Ray.

"I could eat them all up!"

"I tried that," said Clark,

"and I learned something."

"What's that?" asked Billy-Ray Ray.

"When you've had your snack,
just hold back," said Clark.

"That way, everyone gets some."

Mrs. Inkydink smiled.

"Words to live by," she said,

"if I do say so myself."

CLARK THE SHARK'S BITE-SIZED FACTS

1 Sharks use *six* senses to find food. Besides sight, hearing, smell, touch, and taste, sharks can sense electrical fields given off by their prey.

2 Yuck! Sharks *don't* like to eat humans. They would rather eat loads of fish, sea mammals, and plankton!

3 Unlike Clark, sharks eat only when they are hungry. Sometimes days or weeks go by between meals for large sharks.